VIEWPOINTS

A RIGHT TO SMOKE?

EMMA HAUGHTON

W
FRANKLIN WATTS
LONDON • NEW YORK • SYDNEY

First published in 1996 by Franklin Watts
96 Leonard Street, London EC2A 4RH

Franklin Watts Australia
14 Mars Road
Lane Cove
NSW 2066

Series editor: Rachel Cooke
Designer: Nigel Soper, Millions Design
Picture research: Sarah Snashall

A CIP catalogue record for this book
is available from the British Library.

ISBN 0 7496 2381 0

Dewey Classification 362.29

Photographic credits:
b=bottom; t=top; r=right; l=left
Mary Evans Picture Library: pp. 4b, 10b, 28b;
Eye Ubiquitous: p. 12b;
Format: Melanie Friend p. 18t,
Brenda Prince p. 14b;
David Hoffman p. 28t;
Hulton Picture Library p. 11t;
Hutchison Library: Robin Constable p. 10t, Philip
Wolmuth p. 15b,
Melanie Friend p. 29b;
Martin Breese/Retrograph Archive p.8t;
No Smoking Day p. 26t;
Robert Opie p. 6;
Popperfoto pp. 8b, 23b, 25bl, 16;
Rex Features, pp. 5t, 9(both), 11b, 12t, 14t, 17t,
  19t, 20, 21t, 24, 25br, 29t;
Steve Shott cover, pp. 1, 13(both), p.17b, 21b;
Frank Spooner Pictures: Paul Nightingale p. 22;
Science Photo Library: A Glauberman p. 7b, Custom
Medical Stock Photo p. 15t,
Biophoto Associates p. 25tl,
Sygma p. 7t;
Topham Picture Source, pp. 4t, 19b, 23t,
Press Association/Topham, p.27;
Trip: K Cardwell p.5b,
H Rogers p.18b,
A Kuznetsov p.25tr.

Printed in Malaysia

Quotation credits, given from the top of a page beginning with
the left-hand column:
p.5 1 Professor Michael Russell, head of the Addiction Research
Unit, Institute of Psychiatry, London; 2 US President Clinton,
9 August, 1995
p.6 King James I of England and VI of Scotland, 1603
p.7 1 UK Health Eductaion Authority, 1991; 2 Tom Carter
p.8 Bryan Appleyard, Independent, 8 March, 1995
p.9 1 David Simpson, director, International Agency on Tobacco
and Health; 2 Richard Klein, Cigarettes are Sublime
p.10 1 Professor Michael Russell, source as p.5 1; 2 Lisa;
3 Oscar Wilde, 1891
p.12 Americans for Non-Smokers Rights
p.13 1 Jonathan; 2 Bryan Appleyard, Independent, 8 March,
1995; 3 Dr Matin Jarvis, head of the Imperial Cancer Research
Fund's (ICRF) health behaviour unit
p.14 Joanna Smith, mother
p.15 US Environmental Protection Agency (EPA); 2 Americans for
Non-Smokers Rights; 3 Richard Klein, Guardian, 29 May, 1995
p.16 1 UK Health Education Authority; 2 Dr Judith Mackay,
adivser on smoking to Asian governments and health
promotion agencies
p.17 Sir Walter Bodmer, director-general, ICRF
p.18 Tobacco Advisory Council
p.19 1 Paul Thomas, newagent, Brighton, UK; 2 Amanda
Sandford, information manager, Action on Smoking and Health
(ASH)
p.20 Richard Klein, Guardian, 29 May, 1995
p.21 1 Professor Michael Russell, source as p.5 1; 2 Tobacco
Advisory Council
p.22 1 Tobacco Manufacturers' Association; 2 Amanda Sandford,
source as p.19 2; 3 Professor Michael Russell source as p. 5 1
p.23 Freedom Organization for the Right to Enjoy Smoking
(FOREST), UK
p.24 1 Tobacco Advisory Council on government tobacco duty; 2
Martin Jarvis, ICRF, Independent, 31 July 1995
p.26 1 Tom Powney, general manager, Briggs and Shoe Mine,
Independent, 8 September, 1995; 2 Marjorie Nicholson,
spokesperson for FOREST, 10 August, 1995
p.27 1 Dr David Kessler, head of the Food and Drug
Administration; 2 US President Clinton, 9 August, 1995
p.28 1 Dr Martin Jarvis, source as p.13 3; 2 Scott Ballin, head
lobbyist for the US Coalition on Smoking OR Health
p.29 Arnold Trebech, director, US Drug Policy Foundation

Contents

Who smokes?

Humans have smoked tobacco for a long time. There is evidence of smoking in the Maya civilization of Central America, where tobacco originated, as long ago as AD500. It was brought to Europe by the explorers of the 16th century – Sir Walter Ralegh, for example, organized a massive tobacco shipment to England from the West Indies.

However, it was the invention of a machine to manufacture cigarettes at the end of the 19th century that made smoking so widespread in the 20th. Cigarette consumption rose steadily to 1945, when it also became more common for women to smoke. But from the mid-1970s smoking began to decline in many Western countries; in the UK, for instance, just 29 per cent of men smoke now compared with 65 per cent in 1948.

Across the world roughly one third

▲ *Earlier this century smoking was seen as a stylish activity, especially amongst women. As you can see, cigarette holders were all the rage.*

▼ *Sir Walter Ralegh introduced tobacco to England in the 16th century. Some people found the new custom a little unnerving!*

of adults puff their way through five trillion (5,000,000,000,000) cigarettes a year. Over 12.5 million people in the UK and 46 million in the US (26 per cent of the population) smoke, almost equally split between men and women.

While smoking is falling in most Western countries, it is rapidly increasing in Africa, Latin America and Asia. China alone has 300 million smokers. Asia generally is experiencing a smoking epidemic; almost two-thirds of men smoke, with more starting every day. Although currently only 5 per cent of Asian women smoke, that figure is predicted to grow rapidly. This is encouraged by the tobacco companies, who are always on the look out for new markets – British-

olds rose recently to double the government target of 6 per cent. In the US over three million teenagers smoke, with about one million starting every year.

Most smokers start young – some are just three years old when they try their first cigarette. In the US, 80 per cent of adult smokers began before they were 20 years old, with 14 the average starting age. For the tobacco industry these young smokers are the customers of the future. Figures like these prompted US President Clinton to identify underage smoking as one of the greatest threats to health.

66 *Having no teenagers smoke would be one of the easiest, cheapest things to do to change the whole healthcare dynamic in America.* **99**
US President Clinton, August 1995

▼ *Although cigarettes are becoming less popular in rich Western countries, more people are starting to smoke in other parts of the world. In Asia, for instance, almost two-thirds of men now smoke.*

▲ *Studies show that teenage smoking is on the increase, despite government efforts to bring it down. Most smokers begin as teenagers.*

American Tobacco, for instance, announced in 1994 that its next target market would be the former Soviet Union.

Smoking rates tend to be highest amongst the poor. In the UK unskilled working men are three times more likely to smoke than professional men. Some of the highest smoking rates are found among the unemployed.

66 *There's a huge social divide surrounding smoking. The people really killed by smoking are the poor and underprivileged who can't afford things like nicotine replacement treatment to help them give up.* **99**
Professor Michael Russell, head of the Addiction Research Unit, Institute of Psychiatry, London

Smoking is also related to age. While smokers aged 35-49 consume the most cigarettes, it is teenage smoking that is causing most concern. A UK government report found smoking among 11 to15 year

Slow motion suicide?

When Europeans started smoking tobacco in pipes in the 16th century, they were not aware of the risks to their health.

However, some, like King James I of England and VI of Scotland, took an educated guess.

❝ *A custom loathsome to the eye, hateful to the nose, harmful to the brain, dangerous to the lungs, and in the black stinking fume thereof, nearest resembling the horrible Stigian smoke of the pit that is bottomless...* ❞ *King James I of England and VI of Scotland, 1603*

It was not until the 1950s, when cigarettes had become very popular, that doctors began to research links between smoking and lung disease. They did not prove smoking was a cause of lung cancer and chronic bronchitis until 1962, or a major cause of coronary heart disease until the 1970s.

Today the effects of smoking are well known. In each cigarette a powerful drug called nicotine makes the heart beat faster while narrowing the blood vessels and raising blood pressure. Carbon monoxide, also one of the main gases in car fumes, is produced as tobacco burns, depriving the heart of oxygen. Sticky tar from the smoke collects in the lungs. Tobacco smoke contains over 4,000 chemicals, many of them harmful. Just one drop of pure nicotine on your tongue would kill

Craven "A"
FOR YOUR THROAT'S SAKE

◀ *Cigarettes were not always believed to be a health risk. This brand even boasted that it was 'good for your throat'; smoking is now identified as a cause of throat cancer.*

6

▶ *At 120 years old, Jeanne Louise Calment, a French woman, became the oldest person on record in October 1995. She gave up smoking aged 117, only to start again when she was 118!*

you. Other poisons include hydrogen cyanide (used in some US states to adminster the death penalty), arsenic, benzene, formaldehyde, radioactive compounds, pesticides and toxic metals.

Smoking causes 90 per cent of lung cancer, bronchitis and emphysema deaths, and 25 per cent of coronary heart disease deaths. It is linked with cancers of the mouth, throat, oesophagus, bladder, pancreas, kidneys and cervix, and accounts for a third of cancer deaths. Smoking also causes breathlessness, persistent coughs, discoloured teeth and fingers, bad breath and premature wrinkling. However, recent evidence suggests that nicotine may reduce the risk of developing brain disorders like Alzheimer's, Parkinson's and motor neurone disease.

Joe Califano, US Secretary for Health in the 1980s, described smoking as 'slow motion suicide'. The statistics back him up.

❝ *Worldwide it is estimated that by the 2020s, if there is no change in current levels of tobacco consumption, there will be ten million deaths from smoking a year.* ❞ *UK Health Education Authority (HEA)*

In the UK over 115,000 people die from smoking-related diseases every year – roughly one person every five minutes – accounting for nearly a fifth of all deaths. Around 419,000 die yearly in the US. On average smokers lose 10 to 15 years from their lives, with almost half dying before retirement.

Although people are aware of these risks, it does not always stop them smoking.

❝ *I've been smoking for thirty years and I've hardly had a day off sick. A lot of this health stuff is out to scare you, but if it's true, so what? We've all got to die of something.* ❞
Tom Carter, 68

But even tobacco chiefs are not immune: in 1994, R J Reynolds, grandson of the US tobacco company founder, was the fifth Reynolds to die of smoking-related causes.

▶ *The lung on the right belonged to a smoker. Compare it to the non-smoker's lung beside it and you can see the damage done by cigarettes.*

Why start smoking?

Smoking has long been seen as glamorous. In previous centuries cigars and pipes were common items for rich gentlemen; as cigarettes became popular in the 20th century, it gradually became fashionable for both men and women to smoke. Watch any old black-and-white movie, and you will probably see many people smoking.

"*Casablanca* without *cigarettes* is unthinkable; *Casablanca* without cigarettes would be a fascist movie. Plus in every modern war the smoking soldier has been an icon of noble endurance... "
Bryan Appleyard, journalist

Today most Western people are aware of the dangers of cigarettes, and many smokers are trying to give up. In other, poorer, parts of the world, however, cigarettes are associated with more glamorous and wealthy lifestyles – images deliberately fostered by the tobacco companies.

▲ Advertisers have promoted smoking as stylish and elegant for many years, as in this 1920s French advertisement.

Even today, despite all we know about smoking and its dangers, cigarettes still hold an irresistible appeal for many, particularly the young. Smoking is often associated with rock stars, actors or other attractive figures – again, an association subtly

◀ Humphrey Bogart, *Casablanca*'s star, was rarely seen without a cigarette – it was part of his 'tough-guy' image. But smoking brought about Bogart's death of lung cancer at the age of 57.

▲ *The first cigarette, like the first alcoholic drink, is often seen as a beginning of adulthood. You are also much more likely to try a cigarette after a drink, as alcohol lowers your inhibitions.*

promoted by tobacco companies who know that most smokers get hooked in their teens.

Most people hate the taste and sensations of their first cigarette – it is common to feel dizzy or even sick – yet many try again. Why? For young people who live with parents or other relatives who smoke, cigarettes may seem a normal part of growing up. Some teenagers take up smoking because they think it looks cool, sophisticated, or they want to fit in with their friends. For others, it is simply curiosity or a desire to show off. Like trying your first alcoholic drink, smoking is often seen as an introduction to the adult world. Teenagers take up smoking in the belief it makes them look mature; sadly, for most people, it usually suggests the opposite.

After all, is it really glamorous to do something that involves so many health risks? For many the answer is obvious.

66 *For a cosmetics firm to have a model who smokes is a bit like leaving a Rolls-Royce showroom in the hands of a sandpaper salesman.* **99** *David Simpson, director, International Agency on Tobacco and Health, about a leading cosmetic company's choice of model*

Many smokers, however, simply argue that it is a habit they enjoy. Richard Klein, author of *Cigarettes are Sublime*, believes that cigarettes give people a lot of pleasure, and that this is the main reason they choose to smoke.

66 *Tobacco, like alcohol, is a substance in universal use, and must be presumed to have benefits for human civilization if it has been consumed so avidly for so long.* **99**
Richard Klein, Cigarettes are Sublime

But it is a fact that most people who start smoking wish they had not and most want to kick the habit. What begins as a dare or a desire to be accepted can quickly turn into an addiction. And once you are addicted, it can become very difficult to stop.

▼ *For many, smoking continues to have a cool and sophisticated image, despite the health risks. Smoking in films and TV often reinforces this. Here, the actress Uma Thurman is pictured smoking in the 1994 hit movie* **Pulp Fiction***.*

Gasping for a cigarette?

Nicotine, a powerful drug present naturally in tobacco, is highly addictive. When people smoke, nicotine reaches the brain via the lungs in seconds, making them feel more relaxed if they are tense, or more alert and active if they are feeling tired.

Teenagers can become addicted to nicotine very rapidly.

❝ Young people only need to smoke a few cigarettes to have over a 90 per cent chance of becoming a dependent smoker as an adult. You quickly become tolerant to the unpleasant side effects, especially if social pressure makes you keep going. ❞ Professor Michael Russell, head of the Addiction Research Unit, Institute of Psychiatry, London

Although smokers find cigarettes pleasurable, it is not just down to nicotine. Many people find the act of smoking itself comforting in times of stress, or they simply enjoy the ritual of lighting up over a cup of tea or after a meal.

Some people, however, see themselves purely as social smokers, having only the occasional cigarette. They deny that they are addicted.

❝ I sometimes have a cigarette when I'm out, especially if I'm with other smokers. I don't need one the rest of the time. ❞ Lisa, 30

▲ *Relaxing with coffee and cigarettes is a pleasure many people enjoy. However, one sign of addiction in a smoker is that he or she finds it impossible to relax without a cigarette.*

Unfortunately most smokers want to follow one cigarette with another – and another, sometimes only minutes after the last.

❝ A cigarette is the perfect type of the perfect pleasure. It is exquisite, and it leaves one unsatisfied. What more can one want? ❞ Oscar Wilde, 1891

Wilde knew that the effects of nicotine do not last, and as the pleasure wears off, the craving for another cigarette begins. This cycle of addiction leads people to 'chain-

◀ *The famous playwright and renowned wit, Oscar Wilde, understood very well the cycle of addiction that leaves smokers craving another cigarette soon after they have finished their last.*

'Smokers Anonymous' was formed to help smokers to quit in 1956. Meetings like this one must have been a real test of will power.

Alternative therapies such as acupuncture are said to help people give up smoking by easing the craving for a cigarette.

smoke', sometimes up to 40-60 cigarettes a day.

Nicotine is as addictive as heroin, and as hard to give up: seven out of ten smokers have tried to quit and failed at least twice. Those who stop suddenly often feel irritable or nervous and find it difficult to concentrate, especially in the first days. The craving to give in and light up can be very strong indeed. Many people stop for years only to succumb in times of stress or in social situations. It is very hard to stay off cigarettes for good.

Those who do stop enjoy immediate physical benefits.

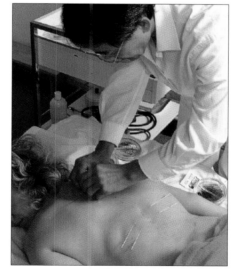

Twenty minutes after the last puff, blood pressure and pulse return to normal. After a day, the lungs start clearing out mucous and other smoking deposits. After two days, the body is clear of nicotine; after

three, breathing becomes easier. Within two to twelve weeks circulation improves; three to nine months later the lungs become more efficient. But it takes five to ten years to halve the risk of heart attack and lung cancer.

Giving up is possible, as 11 million UK ex-smokers can confirm. There are many products available to help, including nicotine replacement gum, patches or lozenges. Some people try dummy cigarettes, filters, even hypnotherapy or acupuncture. But these things help only if you are determined to succeed – the most important factor is willpower.

Whose smoke is it?

Until recently, smoking was seen as an individual choice affecting only smokers themselves. In 1988, however, a report found that those regularly exposed to secondhand cigarette smoke are 10 to 30 per cent more likely to get lung cancer. Non-smokers, who had put up with smoky pubs, offices and restaurants, now had serious cause for complaint.

▼ *Smoky air tends to be an inevitable feature of pubs and bars, but many non-smokers find the smoke irritates their eyes, nose and throat.*

Since then breathing other people's smoke, or passive smoking, has been linked with many health problems, including eye, nose and throat irritation, allergies, bronchitis and lung cancer.

❝Breathing secondhand smoke can aggravate the condition of more than five million Americans with heart disease and 21 million Americans with chronic lung disease. ❞
Americans for Non-Smokers' Rights

It is estimated that at least 1,000 people in the UK and 9,000 in the US die each year from inhaling other people's cigarette fumes. Even pet cats and dogs have been found to suffer skin and chest complaints from their owners' smoking! The US Environmental Protection Agency

❝ *There is no evidence whatsoever of the dangers of passive smoking. It is merely a propaganda device to make smoking a public evil as opposed to a merely private vice. Without the passive smoking scare, there could be no argument against letting smokers kill themselves in peace.* **❞** *Bryan Appleyard, journalist*

But many experts disagree.

❝ *The risk [from passive smoking] is small by comparison with the hazards of active smoking, but real, and it has been recognized by every independent group of scientists to examine the issue.* **❞** *Dr Martin Jarvis, head of the Imperial Cancer Research Fund's (ICRF's) health behaviour unit*

(EPA) now classifies secondhand tobacco smoke as a Group A carcinogen (cancer-causing agent) for which there can be no safe level of exposure.

Only 15 per cent of cigarette smoke is actually inhaled by the smoker – the rest escapes into the surrounding air. Smoke-filled rooms can have up to six times the air pollution on a busy road. Non-smokers breathe in sidestream smoke from cigarettes lying in ashtrays, and mainstream smoke exhaled by smokers; both contain chemicals in high concentrations.

❝ *I can't stand going into smoky pubs or restaurants any more. It's horrible having to eat while people are smoking around you and it makes your eyes sting and your clothes stink.* **❞** *Jonathan, 27*

Passive smokers are now fighting back. In the UK Beryl Roe, who worked for Greater Manchester Council, was recently awarded £25,000 compensation when passive smoking caused chest complaints that forced her out of her job. In 1993 the same council was the first employer to pay compensation to an employee for passive smoking – Veronica Bland, who worked in the same department, won £15,000.

However, the tobacco industry disputes the evidence behind passive smoking – the UK Tobacco Manufacturers' Association claims that 80 per cent of studies found no link between passive smoking and lung cancer, and that any health risks are insignificant. Smokers feel they are simply being harassed.

▶ *Concerns about cigarette smoke in offices have forced many employees to smoke outside.*

VIEWPOINTS

Born to smoke?

Passive smoking is a problem for adults, but much more so for babies and children. Unborn babies are most defenceless – a mother who smokes during pregnancy carries nicotine, carbon monoxide and other harmful chemicals in her bloodstream into that of her baby's. Nicotine makes the baby's heart beat faster, carbon monoxide means he or she gets less oxygen.

The result can be tragic. Babies with smoking mothers are twice as likely to be born dangerously small or too early, and to suffer congenital deformities like cleft lips and palate. They are more likely to die from miscarriage, stillbirth or cot death,

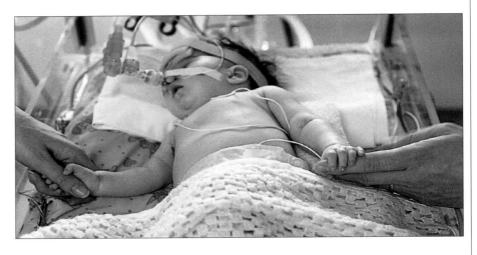

▲ *Babies born to mothers who smoked during pregnancy are more likely to be born prematurely or to have a low birth weight. Lung diseases, such as this baby has, are also more likely and there are higher instances of breathing problems.*

and suffer coughs and breathing problems during their first year. Smoking mothers are themselves at greater risk of pregnancy complications causing bleeding or their waters breaking too early.

Many women who smoke make an effort to stop while they are pregnant. Some find their body helps them.

❝ *In both pregnancies I went off smoking in the first few weeks. Even the smell of cigarette smoke made me feel sick. I knew it was bad for my baby so I was glad I didn't feel like smoking.* **❞** *Joanna Smith, mother*

Once born many babies are exposed to cigarette smoke in their homes. It is estimated that if both parents smoke an average of twenty

◄ *A woman who smokes during pregnancy subjects her baby to harmful chemicals that enter the baby's bloodstream via the placenta.*

and become smoking adults. A recent UK study found that 3 per cent of children under six have tried cigarettes given to them by their parents. Over 60 per cent of children have tried smoking by 15 years old. The younger you start, the greater the risk of health problems later.

But many smokers believe anti-smoking groups have overreacted to the issue of passive smoking.

66 *Humans have lived for 400 years suffused by secondhand smoke. Pregnant women have been smoking and adults blowing it in children's faces for centuries, and yet civilization has survived and possibly flourished.* **99** *Richard Klein, author and journalist*

cigarettes a day, their baby will smoke the equivalent of four packets of cigarettes by the time he or she is a year old. Young children whose parents smoke have twice as many coughs and chest infections, which can cause lasting lung damage by the time they are five.

66 *There is evidence that childhood exposure to cigarette smoke increases the risk of developing cancer as an adult.* **99** *Americans for Non-Smokers' Rights*

Children of smokers are also more likely to try smoking at a young age

▼ Children of smokers may not be so active in the playground. They are also more likely to miss school because of illness.

66 *Environmental tobacco smoke exposure is a risk factor for new cases of asthma in children who have not previously displayed symptoms.* **99** *US Environmental Protection Agency (EPA)*

The EPA estimates that 150-300,000 American children under 18 months get pneumonia or bronchitis every year from breathing secondhand tobacco smoke, and it is well documented that children of smokers take more days off school with illness. But it may not be just their childhood that is affected.

The giants of tobacco?

Since the first cigarette machine was invented over a hundred years ago, tobacco manufacturers have become some of the largest and most successful companies in the world. They have a huge impact on the world economy, wielding considerable power in both Western and developing countries.

The world's six largest cigarette companies are based in the UK and US – Rothmans, British-American Tobacco and Imperial Tobacco in the UK and Philip Morris, R J Reynolds and American Brands, which owns UK subsidiary Gallahers, in the US. In 1994 British-American Tobacco alone made over £1.8 billion profit; in the US tobacco company revenues total around $48 billion a year. Many smaller countries have national companies producing cigarettes for their own people. China, for instance, is one of the largest tobacco producers in the world, but smokes most of the crop itself.

Despite their success, the international tobacco companies are under increasing pressure to find new markets. As the health risks of smoking have become more widely known, the tobacco industry has fought back, first claiming that research into those risks was flawed or irrelevant, then developing low-tar brands to combat falling sales.

However, cigarette sales are still dropping in many Western countries, and new customers need to be found all the time.

> **The tobacco industry needs to recruit 300 new smokers a day just to replace those people killed by smoking attributable diseases.**
> *UK Health Education Authority*

The major tobacco companies are now concentrating many of their resources on selling their cigarettes more widely abroad. They have already had considerable success in many of the world's developing nations, where Western cigarettes have a glamorous image.

> **Young Chinese men in Peking and Shanghai carry Western cigarette packets with two holes: from one they offer Western cigarettes to anyone they want to impress; they use the other for their own local cheap brand to smoke themselves.**
> *Dr Judith Mackay, adviser on smoking to Asian governments and health promotion agencies*

Another strategy to boost profits, adopted by many tobacco companies, is diversifying into other product areas. Philip Morris, which makes Marlboro, the world's best selling brand of cigarettes, also owns General Foods, a company whose

◄ *Philip Morris sponsored ex-UK prime minister Baroness Thatcher's 70th birthday party. In 1992, they hired her to help open up markets in Eastern Europe.*

brands include Maxwell House coffee, Miller Light beer and Jacobs Biscuits. British-American Tobacco owns the UK finance companies Eagle Star and Allied Dunbar.

Indeed, tobacco companies have such a wide presence that many people are investing their money indirectly into cigarettes without realizing it. In the UK, for example, the Imperial Cancer Research Fund recently discovered that £600,000 of the charity's money had been placed

in funds which invest in tobacco company shares.

66 *For the Imperial Cancer Research Fund to have any connection with the tobacco industry is totally unthinkable.* **99** *Sir Walter Bodmer, director-general, ICRF*

▲ *A Russian soldier smokes on a Moscow street in front of an advertisement for an American brand of cigarettes.*

▶ *Many famous brands of household products such as these are owned by tobacco companies. Philip Morris claimed that 10 per cent of money spent on packaged goods in US supermarkets in 1994 was on its goods.*

Nice work if you can get it?

Producing cigarettes is a worldwide industry employing many thousands of people. In the US, for instance, nearly 47,000 people work for the tobacco companies; many thousands more are employed growing tobacco in southern states like Virginia, where it is a traditional crop. Some US farming families have grown tobacco for over 200 years.

Cigarette production is also a significant source of jobs in other countries like the UK.

66 Tobacco manufacturing brings vital economic prosperity to areas of high unemployment, such as Northern Ireland, South Wales, the East Midlands and the North-East; the 11,500 people employed in tobacco manufacturing are among the most productive in the UK. 99
Tobacco Advisory Council

It is not just farmers and factory workers who benefit – sales of cigarettes also provide income for shop owners, for instance. In the UK, independent tobacco sellers count on tobacco sales bringing in 25 to 40 per cent of their turnover and nearly a fifth of their profits.

▲ A tobacco factory in Glasgow in the UK provides employment for these women in an area where jobs can be very difficult to find.

▼ This market selling tobacco leaves in Dubai, United Arab Emirates, is typical of tobacco markets all over the world. Tobacco can be essential to the local economy.

▶ Most cigarettes are sold alongside other goods, but some shops only sell tobacco products.

❝I have to sell a lot of things I don't agree with, like pornographic magazines, sweets loaded with sugar and cigarettes. I can't afford to say no to all these things.❞
Paul Thomas, newsagent

However, in many Western countries jobs in the cigarette industry are becoming more scarce. In the UK, for instance, the number of people employed has dropped from 40,000 in 1979 to about 11,000. The tobacco industry blames these losses largely on rising taxation on tobacco; their opponents say the reduction is mainly due to new technology, as more cigarettes can be produced by fewer people.

Anti-smoking groups argue that discouraging smoking need not lead to more unemployment.

❝*Curbing smoking would reduce jobs only very gradually and give tobacco companies time to diversify into other areas. A major study has shown that a reduction in smoking levels means that people have more money to spend in other areas like leisure, creating more work.*❞
Amanda Sandford, information manager, Action on Smoking and Health (ASH)

Over half the world's tobacco is grown in developing countries like Brazil, India, Turkey and Zimbabwe.

▶ *This tobacco farm is in Zimbabwe, which is one of the largest tobacco growing nations, along with the US, Brazil, India and Turkey.*

Many farmers are under contract to the large multinational tobacco companies, who offer free advice and credit for seed and fertilizer. In addition to subsidising tobacco crops, cigarette companies often set up small local subsidiaries to produce the cigarettes themselves. Labour is much cheaper in poorer countries, and there is a growing market there for cigarettes, as people are less aware of the harmful effects of smoking.

Growing and selling tobacco has definite advantages for developing countries – as well as the help from tobacco companies, they get a guaranteed price for the product. But there are problems, tobacco is a greedy plant which quickly uses up all the nutrients in the soil and needs heavy fertilization; land used for tobacco can become unfit for food production. Some developing countries use up to two-thirds of their agricultural land for tobacco, growing little of their own food and leaving their farmers and their governments relying heavily on the foreign tobacco giants.

Tax to stop smoking?

It is often seen as the government's role to reduce smoking through taxation and health education, yet many governments make a lot of money from smokers. The UK government earned around £8 billion in 1994 in tobacco duty and VAT (value-added tax) on cigarettes, while in 1993 US smokers paid $11.9 billion in cigarette taxes. Three-quarters of the UK price of a packet

▼ *Which sells more cigarettes: the cool advertisement for Death cigarettes that highlights the risks, or the government health warning beneath it? Both could be said to appeal to young people's attraction to 'living dangerously'.*

of cigarettes is tax, making tobacco one of the largest sources of revenue for the government.

By comparison the UK government spends just £10 million a year on anti-smoking health campaigns. Far less will go on smoking education for teenagers, yet ASH estimates that the UK government receives over £80 million in tax on cigarettes sold illegally to under-16-year-olds.

Indeed, the UK government and the European Commission support European tobacco growers through a £936 million annual subsidy to farmers mainly in Italy, Spain and

Greece. It is hardly surprising that many people accuse Western governments of double standards, including those who actually support smokers' rights.

❝ *Governments who want to increase revenues, while they piously protect public health, incite more smoking by enlarging and sharpening these warnings (on the pack). This increases the pleasure for the smoker, on the same principle that leads young smokers to buy Death cigarettes, the package featuring a skull and crossbones.* ❞ *Richard Klein, journalist and author*

▶ *The more cigarettes smoked, the more money governments receive in tax. Some people believe it is not in governments' interests to curb smoking and accuse them of double standards.*

Some people believe there are other incentives for governments which prevent them from clamping down on smoking.

❝*A harsh economist looking at smoking objectively would say it was a good thing. It helps people put up with lousy jobs and finishes them off just as they get to retirement age so they won't go on drawing so much old age pension.* **❞** *Professor Michael Russell, Addiction Research Unit*

However, tobacco companies have a great deal of political influence, putting those politicians who do oppose smoking in a vulnerable position. In the 1970s US Secretary for Health Joe Califano set up a special office on smoking and health to educate the public, but tobacco farmers reacted so strongly that President Carter feared a backlash from the southern states and Califano was forced to resign. Similarly in 1988 former US Surgeon General Dr Everett Koop was refused another term of office, which many felt was due to his campaigning against cigarettes.

Yet government action is vital to discourage smoking. Raising the price of cigarettes by increasing taxation is the most effective way of getting people to cut down or stop altogether – figures suggest a 10 per cent price increase leads to between a 3 and 6 per cent drop in consumption. But the tobacco companies are vehemently opposed to rises in taxation, arguing that it is the poor who suffer most.

❝*It is simply unfair for the Government to expect smokers, a high proportion of whom are in the less well-off groups, to continue to be penalized for choosing to smoke, particularly when the current level of tax is so much higher than other European Community countries.* **❞** *Tobacco Advisory Council*

▼ *On average the money spent on a cigarette in the UK and the USA is divided between government, retailer, advertiser and tobacco company in these percentages.*

AVERAGE PRICE OF A CIGARETTE IN THE U.S. $ 0.13

| Advertising 0.7% | Tax 24.8% | Retailers 5% | Manufacturers 69.5% |

AVERAGE PRICE OF A CIGARETTE IN THE U.K. £ 0.13

| Advertising 1% | Tax 76.91% | Manufacturers 17.1% | Retailers 5% |

Promoting smoking?

Every year the tobacco industry spends huge amounts of money promoting cigarettes – around £100 million in the UK and $340 million in the US alone. Tobacco opponents say the main purpose of advertising is to encourage people to smoke by giving cigarettes a glamorous and exciting image. The tobacco industry, on the other hand, argues that the sole purpose of advertising is to persuade existing smokers to swop brands; one-third of smokers change brands or buy different brands every year.

❝ *There is no convincing evidence to show that tobacco advertising encourages any individual – including children – to start smoking.* ❞ *Tobacco Manufacturers' Association*

While some countries like New Zealand, Canada, Norway and Finland have banned tobacco advertising entirely, most countries restrict it – television adverts, for instance, were banned in the UK in 1965 and the US in 1970. In the UK tobacco advertising is regulated by voluntary agreement – the government and the tobacco industry decides between them how and where tobacco companies can advertise. These agreements do change: recent guidelines state that all shop front cigarette adverts should be removed by 1996, as should adverts on buses and taxis and all those within 200 metres of schools. Some people think these restrictions are not enough.

❝ *Virtually all the medical community believe a ban on tobacco advertising is essential. There's no evidence to show that the voluntary agreements have an impact and where there has been a total ban on cigarette adverts, it has led to a reduction in smoking.* ❞ *Amanda Sandford, information manager, ASH*

Despite the fact that cigarette adverts are not allowed to appeal directly to young people, many worry

▼ *This advert for the UK Benson and Hedges brand is deliberately cryptic. It is not obvious what product they are selling but perhaps it also implies it is 'clever' to smoke.*

that they encourage children to take up smoking. They argue that tobacco promotion sends children confusing messages – how can smoking be unacceptable if adverts glamorize it?

❝ *Young people know what these adverts are about far more often than adults.* ❞ *Professor Michael Russell, Addiction Research Unit, on the brand advertisements which feature cryptic visual jokes*

As advertising restrictions have increased, tobacco companies have relied more heavily on sports sponsorship, worth over £10 million a year in the UK alone. Sponsorship has the advantage of associating cigarettes with sporting excellence and glamour, and can give longer television coverage than direct advertising. Opponents argue that

PERFECTLY SUITED? (4,2,7)

13mg TAR 1·1mg NICOTINE
SMOKING CAUSES HEART DISEASE
Health Departments' Chief Medical Officers

Sweet & Cool

PLAYERS
NAVY CUT CIGARETTES

10 for 6ᵈ
50 for 2/5

20 for 11½
100 for 4/8

PLAYER'S NAVY CUT

◀ *Tobacco manufacturers often try to associate cigarettes with an active lifestyle. This 1923 advert for Player cigarettes was made when the dangers of cigarettes were virtually unknown, and would be unlikely to be allowed today.*

▼ *As restrictions on cigarette advertising increase, sports sponsorship has become more important to the tobacco companies, as it can reach a wide audience through television coverage of events. The sponsorship does raise money for sport, but many sports are now refusing to have their name associated with cigarettes.*

this is advertising 'by the back door' – according to the UK Health Education Authority, two-thirds of children aged 9 to 15 claim to see cigarette advertising on television.

The smoking industry disagrees, saying many sports rely on the money raised by sponsorship to stage events. Moreover, the pro-smoking lobby believes stringent restrictions on advertising are not only ineffective but also a form of censorship, denying companies the right to promote their products.

" *In relatively free market economies like Thailand, Taiwan, Singapore, Iceland, Italy, Norway, Finland and Sweden, despite the imposition of bans, total and per capita cigarette consumption has risen in all these countries.* **"** *Freedom Organization for the Right to Enjoy Smoking (Forest), UK*

Too high a price to pay?

Life for smokers can be expensive. An average UK smoker starting at 20-years-old will spend over £40,000 before retirement – the cost of a house in many areas of the country. Unfortunately, the price of smoking often hits the poorest hardest.

> *It is estimated that 20 per cent of the UK's poorest households pay more tobacco tax than income tax, yet the government seems content to continue to ask smokers to pay out more than their fair share.*
> Tobacco Advisory Council on government tobacco duty

Yet it is often the poor who find it hardest to stop.

> *Half of the most affluent smokers have now given up but only 5 per cent of the most deprived have done so. Seventy per cent of the people who can least afford it still smoke.*
> Martin Jarvis, ICRF

Smoking can be an expensive habit, but many people are prepared to pay for the relief it brings from stress and boredom – and quitting can also be costly. In the UK, for example, nicotine replacement patches, proven to increase the chances of stopping successfully, cost around £190 for a full course.

Not everything, however, is more expensive for smokers. While life assurance can cost up to 40 per cent more, one UK assurance company now offers smokers higher retirement incomes on some pension funds. Why? Because it knows from research and statistics that regular smokers are likely to die sooner.

But the cost of cigarettes does not just fall on individuals. In the UK, for instance, 50 million working days a year are lost through smoking-related illness, while lost working days cost American employers $8.4 billion annually. Smokers at work waste an average of a day a week taking smoking breaks. The US Department of Health and Human

▶ Cigarettes are probably one of this homeless man's greatest expenses. But it is far harder to kick the habit when living on the breadline.

▲ The cost of health care is huge and, with money scarce, some doctors have refused to treat people with smoking-related diseases.

▶ This Siberian worker's cigarette break costs his company time – and money. At ten minutes a cigarette, breaks soon add up.

Services put 1993 smoking-related medical costs at $50 billion, while the UK National Health Service spends over £500 million annually on smokers' diseases.

Smoking also drains global resources. A modern cigarette machine, for example, uses over six kilometres of paper an hour. One tree is burnt in the process of curing and drying enough tobacco to be rolled into 300 cigarettes – around a tree a fortnight for the average smoker. This results in the felling of 5-11 million acres of forest every year. Each day UK smokers throw away 300 million butts and 20 million cigarette packets.

Many fires are started by cigarettes. The UK Home Office puts smokers' materials as the second highest cause of accidental fires in the home, causing 6,200 in 1993. Many forest and scrub fires are also caused by careless smokers.

◀▲ One of the UK's worst fires, at King's Cross underground station in 1987, was started by a match or cigarette – it killed 31 people and led to a smoking ban on the London Underground.

What is being done?

Most Western countries have campaigns against smoking, usually aiming to educate people about the dangers of smoking and force governments to restrict the tobacco industry in areas like advertising.

Increasing public awareness of the health risks is a major area for anti-smoking campaigners. National no-smoking days are now common, and health warnings compulsory on every cigarette and rolling tobacco packet. The discovery of a link between passive smoking and disease has added fuel to the campaigners' fire – smoking is now banned in many public places, including public transport, shops, restaurants and schools.

Some individuals are tackling the tobacco industry head on. In 1988 in New Jersey, USA, Anthony Cippolone succeeded in getting $400,000 compensation from a tobacco company when his 58-year-old wife Rose died of lung cancer – the first time a tobacco company has been found liable for a smoker's death.

Many private companies are now also taking action, banning smoking in the workplace or restricting it to certain areas. One UK shoe shop chain even pays its non-smoking workers 15 pence an hour more than their smoking colleagues.

▲ *No-smoking days are a popular and effective way of drawing the public's attention to the benefits of giving up.*

NO SMOKING

❝ *The non-smoking bonus has been an integral part of the business plan. We have a healthier and fitter staff and it has cut down absences.* **❞**
Tom Powney, general manager, Briggs and Shoe Mine, quoted in a UK newspaper

Some smokers, however, see work restrictions as an infringement of personal liberty.

❝ *Who the hell do these people think they are? If a policy to ban all smoking inside and outside buildings is allowed it would set a precedent saying that employers can stipulate the lifestyle of their employees.* **❞**
Marjorie Nicholson, spokesperson for FOREST

◀ *No smoking signs are simple and easy to recognize. They are also becoming more common in public places.*

▶ Anti-smoking campaigns often enlist the support of celebrities, particularly from the health-conscious world of sport. Here soccer stars, Robbie Earl and John Fashanu, promote no smoking with school children.

The US government has recently become more active in trying to curb smoking. The Food and Drug Administration (FDA), which regards cigarettes and their nicotine content as a drug which needs regulating, has threatened to ban cigarettes if the agency is not allowed to control tobacco.

❝ *The public may think of cigarettes as no more than blended tobacco rolled in paper, but they are more than that. Some of today's cigarettes may, in fact, qualify as high-technology delivery systems that deliver nicotine in quantities sufficient to create and to sustain addiction in the vast majority of individuals who smoke regularly.* ❞
Dr David Kessler, head of the FDA

President Clinton and the FDA have unveiled new steps aimed to halve underage smoking, including a ban on cigarette vending machines, further restrictions on advertising, and a proof-of-age requirement when buying tobacco. Although these moves could lead to the loss of up to 1,000 tobacco jobs a year, the US government seems determined to carry them through.

❝ *We need to act, and we must act now before another generation of Americans is condemned to fight a difficult and gruelling personal battle with an addiction that will cost millions of them their lives.* ❞
President Clinton, August 1995

But are governments simply following the mood of the times? More and more non-smokers are now prepared to fight for their right to clean air, even if that just means approaching smokers in no-smoking zones and asking them politely to put out their cigarette.

Should smoking be banned?

Should we have the right to choose whether to smoke? Tobacco, like alcohol, was around long before anyone was aware of the risks. A ban would be difficult to enforce, as proved by the US prohibition on alcohol earlier in the century. On the other hand, many drugs like cannabis have already been classed as dangerous and made illegal.

Smokers and non-smokers are caught in a deadlock about our freedom to smoke. Some believe no-smoking bans have gone too far. In New York, a silhouette of the former

▲ Anti-smoking campaigners argue that addiction restricts personal liberty: a smoker is a prisoner of his or her addiction.

▼ Smuggled alcohol is poured down the drain in the US during the Prohibition era. Banning alcohol proved impossible to enforce. Banning smoking might cause similar problems.

president Franklin D. Roosevelt which shows him smoking has been removed as it is believed it may encourage smoking. Smokers argue, like the slogan on the UK Philip Morris advert, that "the passion to regulate down to the finest detail of people's lives can lead to infringements of personal liberty".

However, those opposed to tobacco are equally steadfast.

❝ Smokers' inability to quit despite wanting to and in the face of proven smoking-related disease is the biggest restriction of personal liberty. ❞ Dr Martin Jarvis, ICRF

As we gain more information about the risks to smokers and non-smokers alike, campaigns to curb

cigarettes are gaining momentum. Current policies appear to favour the anti-smokers.

❝ Smoking is not going to go away overnight... [but] the prospects are better than they have been in 30 years. ❞ Scott Ballin, head lobbyist for the US Coalition on Smoking OR Health

Many countries are adopting or tightening restrictions on advertising and promotion of cigarettes, smoking in public places, and the sale of tobacco. According to the World Health Organization, a third of schools and places of entertainment

are smoke-free, as are half of public places and nearly half of health care services.

Most countries restrict access to cigarettes by young people, although this is not always effective – ASH estimates that UK children, for instance, smoke over 800 million cigarettes a year. Some Muslim countries have banned smoking outright. However, in many countries even those strongly opposed to tobacco are reluctant to see it outlawed, believing it would drive cigarettes, like drugs, underground.

66 *We would have a black market in cigarettes that would make the current black market in cocaine and heroine look like a Sunday-school picnic.* 99 *Arnold Trebech, director, US Drug Policy Foundation*

Indeed, it is estimated that a third of the world's cigarettes are already smuggled. In Europe alone, more than 50 billion cigarettes 'disappear' each year, leading to huge sums of lost revenue for governments.

Anti-smoking organizations like ASH suggest that instead of imposing bans we should, like Canada and New Zealand, adopt a package of measures to reduce smoking, including health education and support to quit, high taxes on cigarettes, a ban on advertising and promotion, more smoke-free areas, and tighter controls on underage smoking.

As long as cigarettes are so profitable, it is unlikely that they will ever be banned completely, however damning the health evidence against them. This leaves us all with a very personal choice about whether or not to smoke. Each one of us must weigh up all the facts – for and against – and make our own decision. Is smoking worth it?

▼ *Smuggling cigarettes is estimated to lose governments more than £10,000 million a year. However, others gain: these cigarette boys live by trading on the black market in Albania.*

Glossary

ACUPUNCTURE: A Chinese therapy involving piercing the skin with needles at certain points in the body. It can be used to treat various illnesses and to relieve pain as well as to help with nicotine addiction.

ADDICTION: A physical or mental dependency on a habit or substance; a strong desire to repeat doing or taking something, particularly drugs.

ARSENIC: A deadly poison that has been traditionally used in murders.

BENZENE: A gas and common constituent of petrol. It is known to cause cancer.

BLOOD PRESSURE: The pressure of the blood on the walls of the blood vessels. It is used as a common indicator of health, with prolonged high blood pressure increasing the chances of heart attacks.

BRAND: A name of a product given to it by its makers. Marlboro or Silk Cut are well-known brands of cigarette.

BRONCHITIS: An inflammation of the air tubes, which branch into the lungs from the windpipe.

CARBON MONOXIDE: A colourless, odourless and very poisonous gas found in car exhaust. It can kill by depriving the body of oxygen.

CENSORSHIP: The supression, usually by government, of certain literature, speech or materials.

CHAIN SMOKING: This describes the habit of continuously smoking one cigarette after another.

CONGENITAL DEFORMITY: A handicap or physical problem present from birth.

EMPHYSEMA: A lung condition that distends the lungs and causes breathing difficulties.

FORMALDEHYDE: A poisonous chemical. It is often used in preserving biological specimens.

HYPNOTHERAPY: A therapy involving hypnosis which can be used to help with nicotine addiction.

LIFE ASSURANCE: An insurance taken out by a person to give financial benefits to relatives in the event of his or her death.

MAINSTREAM SMOKE: This is the smoke breathed out by someone smoking.

NICOTINE: A powerful and highly poisonous drug. It is the main chemical responsible for the addictive quality of cigarettes.

PASSIVE SMOKING: Breathing in other people's cigarette smoke.

PNEUMONIA: A serious inflammation of the lungs that can lead to death.

PLACENTA: The organ that develops in a woman's womb during pregnancy. It supplies the baby with the food it needs for development.

SIDESTREAM SMOKE: This is the smoke given off by cigarettes when they are alight but not being actively smoked.

SPONSORSHIP: The system by which a company gives money to a sport or an event in return for displaying its name or logo so it is seen by any audience watching.

TOBACCO: The leaves of the plant *nicotiana tabacum* and the main ingredient in cigarettes. Tobacco is a natural source of nicotine.

TOBACCO DUTY: A tax imposed by governments on tobacco products as a means of raising revenue. Tobacco tax is also used as a way of discouraging smoking. Adding more tax increases the price of cigarettes, which gives people a greater incentive to stop.

VALUE-ADDED TAX: VAT is a tax added by some governments to the price of many goods and services and paid by the puchaser. It is currently set in the UK at 17.5 per cent of the product price.

Useful Addresses

UK

ASH - Action on Smoking and Health
109 Gloucester Place
London W1H 4EJ
Tel: 0171 935 3519

Cancer Research Campaign
10 Cambridge Terrace
London NW1 4JL
Tel: 0171 224 1333

Health Education Authority
Hamilton House
Mabledon Place
London WC1H 9TX
Tel: 0171 383 3833

QUIT
Victory House
170 Tottenham Court Road
London W1P 0HA
Tel: 0171 388 5775
Quitline: 0800 00 22 00

Tacade (The Advisory Council on
Alcohol and Drug Education)
1 Hulme Place
The Crescent
Salford M5 4QA
Tel: 0161 745 8925

Tobacco Advisory Council
Glen House, Stag Place
London SW1E 5AG
Tel: 0171 828 2041

Australia

Australian Commonwealth Health
Service
120 Sussex Street
Sydney 2000

Benson & Hedges Co P/L
77 Paramatta Road
Silver Watee 2141

Cancer Council
153 Dowling Street
Woolloommooloo 2011

Facts to think about

◆ Tobacco costs the UK National Health Service over £500 million a year for treating smoking-related diseases. The government gets ten times that amount in tax on cigarettes.

◆ Over 400,000 Americans die from smoking every year.

◆ About a quarter of 17- and 18-year-old Americans smoke.

◆ Greece has the highest life expectancy in Europe despite being the heaviest smoking nation in the world.

◆ At least 50 million working days are lost to UK industry every year from smoking-related sick leave.

◆ In 1994 smoking giant BAT Industries, one of the largest companies in the UK, made profits of £1.8 billion.

◆ Every year about 500 billion cigarettes are smoked in the US.

◆ In the UK smoking kills over six times as many people as road and other accidents, murder, manslaughter, suicide, illegal drugs and AIDS all put together.

◆ In 1989 smoking was banned on virtually all US internal flights.

◆ Over 11,000 British people are employed by tobacco companies.

◆ Of those Americans who smoke, at least 70 per cent would like to quit but only 2.5 per cent manage each year.

◆ The UK Office of Population, Censuses and Surveys defines a smoker as person who smokes one or more cigarettes a week.

Index